For my family, friends, and supporters. May our lives prosper together. To my lover, whomever you may be, may our love kindle to something wonderful.

Nevaeh Frazee

Your dreams are wild child,
Don't let them be
It's that young love, wild child,
Young love that'll set you free

1.

You are tired

You are sad

You are lonely

I was weird,
Or so how you described it,
For wanting to be loved so much
As if it were a burden to you
I only ask to be loved
Because I faced too many who
Didn't, and spit on a promise by lying
And cheating
And assaulting me
You are not like them,
But I needed to be reminded
So I didn't lose you
To my imagination
And would have to fabricate you
Telling me I was beautiful in my dreams
When I begged for it
To be a reality

~ *N. f.*

Don't fall for it
Don't get trapped into someone
Who could never love you
As much as you love him
Don't do it
Don't do i
Don't do
Don't d
Don't
Don'
Don
Do
D
Do
Do y
Do yo
Do you
Do you l
Do you lo
Do you lov
Do you love
Do you love m
Do you love me
Do you love me n
Do you love me no
Do you love me now
Do you love me now?

　　　~N. f.

Please, heart, spare me
Another heartbreak
For a lost soul,
I can't break anymore
Than I already have
Don't enslave me to another
I cast my life away to only
Tumble off the deck and drown
In the ocean
O' my heart, never to bob the
Surface of the icy water
To be caught again
Forever embedded in the
Black sand where it shall
Sleep in a never-returning
Slumber, unbreakable,
Without itself to vie the
Fish that slit away from
The beat beat beat
Of a love still living

~N. f.

And suddenly
I was daydreaming about you
The poetry became your figure
And your smile became the
Only thing before my eyes

But I am not on your mind
You are somewhere else
With your life
And I am here
Waiting
For you to return
Back to me

False hopes
Will burn me alive
If your ignorance
Doesn't first

~N. f.

I love you
And you loved me
See the difference?

I *love* you
And you *loved* me
And those two things
Are built entirely differently

~N. f.

It is the tooth bearing
Monster that caves in at dawn
The snarl lurking in the corner
Of their eyes
And the bladed beast
That paces hungrily at night
It is the temptation that there is
More beyond than we comprehend
But it is the last barrier we have to break
We are filed down to one dimensional
Beings floating past our colleagues
And chained to its grasp
It tethers us to believe our feet
Are made of stone and our energy
Blows away in the wind
So even with a sword we can't
Hurt the demon drenched inside
Our souls
As we try to fight it by purging our skin
To attempt to bleed it out
It is the silent monster that
Shreds our throats and burns our eyes
To try and stop us from speaking out
And seeing what we could be without it
It is the knife we hide every day
And pretend we can breathe but slowly,
It plunges

~N. f.

The unflattering whisper from him
Continues to haunt me
The devil-n'-angel voice that
Heeds me to my upmost
Greatest lengths to separate
Me from our fantasy
This cacophonous dream stalks me
At night, conversing with my reality
And the one I wish I had
It asks me what I could do
To retake the lies I was fed
And combust it into the perception
Of which truth and dystopian are
Opposing parallels within the grey

~N. f.

I was engulfed in the lips pressed to mine
As we created this fantasy
So shallow you were that you drank
The sea from my tongue and drained
The life from my craving eyes
I was wanting to feel loved
But you took all of mine from every
Inch, feeding venomous poison that
Sank deep into my veins
And leaving me a desert in the
Patience of rain, never to witness
A drop from you
Here, contemplation holds so dangerous
When you have no sanction to turn to
And when the shadows creep from
The floor and shake the carpet
Beneath every moral you tower upon
And when the stature has bled
You blame me for the stains
On your hands
And the stoic countenance I pity
On the smug, deceiving features of your face

~N. f.

My limits have exceeded
Far beyond my stony breach
The cobblestone chisled and crumbled
By the picks of scrawny
Hungry men with scraggly fangs
And wolf snarls behind their darting eyes
I am cumbersome to the likes
Of death fitting my silhouette
Dressed up with the scars
From the moon hunters
That remain to only crawl from the
Darkness when provoked by my fresh
Blood and the sweet pears that
Blossom from my chest
They tirelessly rampage when I brush them
From my surface, and bury deep within
My caverns of a womanly empire
So may I salvage the shreds I
Can spare from the carnage?
I might seek someone to enter the
Collusion of my being and make
Me enlightened beyond my passion
Yet I am a prisoner shackled to the
Knuckles of these moon hunters
And called to wake from my slumber
To the convenience of their judgement
Shall I slut my way to their shallow
Hearts and my figure the only thing
That gleams in their esteemed presence

~N. f.

In a uniform world
I would never again teeter my strength
I would feel knowingly validated
I could be loved endlessly
By those that hurt me, in turn, would
They would step aside their selfish temperaments
And never cross my step again

For how selfish am I to ask to be loved
As I do the world?
What man would drive his lovers
To suicide— I may not know, but
It has happened— prolonged for years
The dead eyes peer from walking
Corpses— and beg to be nullified of
Existence— and tirelessly aim on
In a scalar projection—unknowing
Arriving somewhere
Lost, contemplate, longing
A holy grail in his frame that he
Refuses to tip
A masked language no being dares
To utter to the wind; all-knowing it be
That death would catch the whispers
And listen more than life
Hungry as they are to exempt themselves
From the destruction raging their mind

~N. f.

I hate you
And I don't hate anyone
Yet I hate the one who pushed
His way past my *no* and inside
My womanhood anyways
I hate the one that got me
Intoxicated and unable to recall
How I got those bruises on my thighs
I hate the one who controlled
My clothes and my friends
And went about kissing her
I hate the one who promised
He'd never cheat on me
That she was the last one
In line past three other women
I hate them for taking my
Purity and kindness, as they tried to freeze
Me so I'd be as cold as they are
But what they don't know is
I've thawed through their torment
Every
Single
Time

~N. f.

My countenance dimmed
There was nothing more to say
To a lover who refuses to stay

~*N. f.*

Don't you dare blame this heartbreak
On me, for the responsibility of your actions
Are wretched by you and you alone
I am not the one to sacrifice to your demons
Because I am handling some of my own

~N. f.

I do not doubt what you did to me
Was assault
This victim's guilt depresses me
Was there something I could've done?
Why did I let it happen?
Will anyone actually believe me?
Will I finally be happy?
Will they suffer like I have?
It's all so sickening how I've
Succumbed to me being a victim
I am instead a survivor—
A warrior—
To battle what crosses my way
And to never let it destroy me like this again

~N. f.

Deleted him from social media
His photos all erased
But the portraits in my head still remain
The fingerprints on my skin
My shoulders, my waist
And his hand burned around my
Soft fingers still tell me
I have not forgotten him
I could scrub myself raw
Until I bled and his prints
Would still be embedded in my bones
So I mustn't pick at the scabs
Let my wounds heal
And make room for another
Love to enter my world

~N. f.

With people
I have achieved a deep need for personal
Congruency and for healthy, growing
Relationships
The problems they have made have
Met tremendous cost
I don't know myself and
I've had to ask myself
Is it worth it?
I've studied myself after a few weeks
And I just can't seem to be
Friendly, to myself or others, anymore

~N. f.

The ring ring ringing of his voice
And I beg for one more word
Stay
Love
You are beautiful
You are the best thing to happen to me
But as a lake waiting for a full moon
When it is masked behind the clouds
I am waiting for something
That will never appear

~N. f.

Love will always be my greatest hinder
Not because I refuse to love

I refuse to not be loved back

~N. f.

I am burning burning burning
A fire cannot be doused
When you're dangling the water
Tantalizingly above my head
Just out of reach
Please just whisper a few drops
You are beautiful
You are my happiness
I love you more
My heart burns burns burns
And you stand there
Watching my demise
 - Heart burn

 ~N. f.

You were the one
I wanted to impress with my poetry
Every syllable
Every letter
I carved into symphonies
You drove me crazy
In only the way a writer
Can never stop writing for
So this love never meets an ending
You ignited the words in me
As easily as fall leaves graced
The ground and the colors
Lit up the world like you lit
Up mine

~N. f.

I love too much
To be treated like I don't matter
I need more
And if you can't give it
Then *walk away*

~N. f.

You were compelling, my love

Beauty in the tradgedy

That became

Of us

~N. f.

Just see me
Look at me
My eyes
My thighs
My cries
For you to look up
And see what I've become
At the hands of your ignorance

   ~N. f.

I need love
I crave for you to see how
Beautiful I am
And to love it all
Not *this*
Not ignore all that I am
Not play your games
My voice to only be a mere buzz
Not chase the dragon
Of what I cannot be
Don't say that you can't give affection
When that's all you seem
To give to *her*

~N. f.

And you left me

Like you always do

Like they've all done, too

~N. f.

It was a masterpiece
You and I
The colors danced around us
As we thrived together
And drained to a bleak grey
When you left

~N. f.

How could I ever forget you?
You're the one that put the
Words in my mouth and poured
All over the pages
Soaking with the essence
And the last goodbye
Of you

~N. f.

We had our storms
But you were always the one
That locked me out in the rain

~N. f.

The pan on the cubicles faces
The longing gazes into nothing
Dressed in fashion easily representable
Differently and equally alike
All zoned out into the void
Inside the walls we tame the colors
With the brown desks we bang on
We hate on
We slate on, write on, take on

~N. f.

The space is my arms isn't
Large enough to hold my heavy heart
Yet I will carry these burdens anyway
As my love is just something tossed away
But I don't see anyone here to release my mind

~N. f.

I wasn't a lonely soul only;
I was teething at the crumbs
Thrown from inattentive sweethearts
And battling myself against the thought
That I deserved nothing

He was the one who showed me
How deep my ocean caverened
And swam from top to bottom
Leaving memories printed on the tissue
Forever
Now he has left, and I am one empty,
Massive sea no other has been brave
Enough to dive into like he did
Not a single soul could ever reach
The parts of me like he would with ease
And the consequences for trusting someone
Deep into my waters
Has left me desolate and too full
For it seems no one could handle my vastness
As beautifully as he did

~N. f.

He might have felt nothing
But I felt everything
More than enough for both him and I combined
So that he could continue to feel nothing
Like he desired
And I could feel everything
Just how I imagined
Is that fair?
It was the way the pieces
Fell that night

~ N. f.

Day one
The counselor's office was chilly
My tears almost froze on my cheek
As he took my statement
They both watched me collapse in my seat
Unable to utter a breath
And I wondered if they thought I was
The girl with the case that would
Change the world
I thought I was the collateral embodiment
Of a victim attempting to find her voice
Talking, but not fully heard

Day four
The weekend crawled on
And Monday came forth the deputy
The bearer of questionings that didn't
Seem to end, but circle in a whirlwind
To fabricate my story
My statements
My pain
Onto a case file
From emotions came words
And soon would come actions
But all were meddled down to the core
And plastered to only a number
A number that would not leave
To the left of my name
My new identification

Day five
The therapy room was comforting
The walls whispered condolences
But did not take pity on me
Here, plop!, I vented to every object that would
Lend a listening ear
I absorbed, so deeply, into my being
As the therapist and I soul searched
And embedded the purple light in my veins
But recalled the red that seeped into my marrow
Deep in the tissue
The moments that jumped to and fro my sight
And pitter-pattered against the coarse pain
Ghostly
From my pelvis, and my breasts, and my
Lips, and my neck
The image of his multi-colored canvas blanket
As he penetrated deep into my womanhood
The sole rock of support for my defense
And the connector to my assault
This blanket, reminded me of my childhood
What should shroud me from harm
Watched emptily, looked on with sorrow
And turned aid away from my reach
Oh, how I wanted to cover myself from him

They say love is complicated
And one wrong tweak
Could make the entire contraption
Dissipate into a pile of a mess
Love is indeed a masterpiece
Complicated in the rough details
The hours and days and years
Spent on crafting dreams with
Paint brushes
And fixing the mistakes
That will always be impressions
Underneath the colors painted over it;
All of this time
Will reveal
Watercolor stories of
Two souls
Who worked together
Lovingly adding strokes to the canvas
Each day together
And we'll demonstrate how love
Will always remain
A beautiful thing

~N. f.

The pen remembers all
Of the nights I frivolously
Scribbled out love poetry
And on the other hand
Shakily wrote my broken heart
Into words on this canvas
The pen is my instrument
Of the construction and destruction
In my world
And prevails to be my
Longest friend
I nurture the poetry
And it heals me through
Each line, dash, and period
I feed it
Hungry and beckoning for more
Stories to line each page
Of a proud and true
Masterpiece
To become

~N. f.

She is out there
At 13 years old
14 years old
15 years old
16 years old
Connecting with the poetry
Of heartbreak
Of loss
Of sexual assault
And the portrayal that
Depression is trendy

Mental illness has too many times
Been shoved through shows
And movies
And music
That it has become
Driven into these generations
That the sad girl
Will get the prince
Not the strong one
Not the leader
Not the one who's looking
To grow
Teaching them to be submissive
Where in a real world
We need leaders
And strength from the media
To teach these men and women
To get help with their emotions

And not to follow down
The rabbit hole of
Detrimental and harmful
Mindsets and behavior

~N. f.

Sometimes the person
We need to listen to
Is our own advice
We give others

~N. f.

You wouldn't accept
A rose halfway bloomed

Don't do the same thing
With their halfway love

~N. f.

It's easy to write about the lonely
Corners of a heart
It's more difficult to accept the
Breathing, beating whole of it
It's easy to write about the pain
And be at loss with the bliss
But there will be days to come
To learn and gaze contently
Upon the beauty
The universe gifted you with

~N. f.

My eyes scream the thunder
My lips are the storm
If I told you my heart
I'd let it all pour
Until I'm ripped apart
From dangling chords
Your eyes would grow hard
And your mind would be sore
The air would be full
And you'd let it all drain
I'd be silent until
You say let's never meet again
The thunder would brew
And ignite the rain
I'd let you in my shelter
And you'd burn it to the frame
So quietly I go
Rest another day
To the heartbeat of yours
In my strength I'll restrain
And the night goes on,
On, on, on, on

~N. f.

The emotionally unavailable
And the physically distanced
Have been where my heart
Has led me to
The festering trouble
Budding like flesh wounds
Picking at the scabs off that
Scathing scar tissue I've dressed
With men
Are unlike him
He who laces his fingers
Through my hair and
Holds me dear
To his own scars,
Pressing me like aloe to the
Pain of the past to patch
His memories as if to awaken
From a nightmare he leads to
Forget in the fog of amnesia
My embrace lingers upon him
And I would call to do the same
But he is all too close
And too real
To let myself be forgotten
Against the peeling rickets of flesh
My worldly history bestows upon me
To let myself become attached
To another lover
Once more

~N. f.

Of pinnacle sprouts sayings
The woes of children ever growing
Lit schoolyards designed by the outdated
And hurtled from these generations
"Thou's opinion meets hark
For a child's hands cannot furl
The trigger of a glock
And the light cannot mural
The babbled brains of the confused—
Trust in them, we cannot"
For what good does the youth present
In the leadership's resentment
Us children of the Lord repent
Tradition and must be guided by
The clutches of Satan
Yet we are the stature
Waiting to blossom from the
Repressed soil and bury
The faithless under the shadows

~N. f.

And what if the world fell
In love with you?

I did, under summer skies
I did, when you couldn't bear
The way the mirror snarled at you
I did, with all the stars in my hands
As they watched you bury yourself
In the pain of everyday nuisance
I did when I wrote the poetry
The sad, tormented, longing lines
In midnight reprise
I did as I crushed my soul
To heal yours
I did fall in love with the perfect
Person who stared at me with
Emptiness, for you loved the way
My poetry fell to your feet,
As I lost my mind

~N. f.

I felt like a library
With the way you read my mind
And wrote notes in the margins
With a lovely soft smile

~N. f.

The clouds peered from the gaze
Of the moon, whose light shone
On all of the broken hearts
That longed to be reborn
Happy and loved

~N. f.

You have to let him go
You *must*

His Saturday night plans are not
Part of your life, nor you are not his anymore
To plan for
You must cut him loose to not let
His actions carry the way you smile
And cry at night wondering what you
Could have done better

Let him go darling
And leave him be

~N. f.

Sometimes the ones you love the most
Hurt you to the core
Shake your morals
Question your being
But you are worth the love
They cannot give

~N. f.

Kill your albatross
Shake that heavy weight off
Your chest and breathe
My darling

~N. f.

You remind me of simpler times
When I could just live
In perfect harmony
Without a worry
And care free

~N. f.

Keep me quiet, they wished,
But I roar with the waves
That crash down upon those that silence me

~N. f.

Our expectations are our downfall
You need the roses
But I need them without thorns
You need the darkness
I need the light

~N. f.

The greatest challenge in history
Has always been going against
What others deem to be wrong

~N. f.

I was consumed with a desire to succeed
Our roles can do so little
To great lengths
And exponential wonders

~N. f.

A bird swoon, a sigh,
A daisy petal amongst the wings
And fall as if it never appeared
These amongst other beautiful things
And the a calamity in such a reprise
That the lonely beggars will comprehend
Temporary beautiful for all it consumes
In a world too full of pretend

~N. f.

He watches with temptation
In the show I play
Dance beautiful
I shine under the spotlight
My skin glistening glitter
Gleaming in my eyes
He sways with my movement
In the midnight, we rise
To a paradox song of love
And mourn the lost with love

    ~N. f.

In a world where chaos is
Grown exponentionally
We expect there to be understanding
Outside and within
But there is none
And we wonder why this is
The only language we all comprehend
Is love

~N. f.

I wondered when you'd notice
Just how far the take away grew from us
What I'd become after you left me
And what you'd lose to another
I wonder just how much you miss me
But I do not wish your presence to be back
Never again will I sacrifice my grin
To seal up the harmful poisonous veins
That don't wish to seek remedy

~N. f.

Do not ask me
Where I have traveled to find you
Because my path has not been a smooth
Prairie in the basking light
It was cavernous, disastrous, cacophonous
In the sense that I couldn't find my way
Not until you came
And until I found my being along the alleyways
That stalked me until I became dizzy
And sick with longing resolution
To finally become one path
With you

~N. f.

I'm sailing alongside his
Stoic figure, budding with flowers
Against his brood chest, but so
Delicate they become while he breathes
He is steel; a barricaded stronghold for
The world on the outside of his fleshy,
Soft and sweet heart he let's me hold
Every minute or two, I would never dream
Of crushing the vessels in my fist as
He cautiously watched me handle something
He's taken so long to heal
I thank him for letting me hold the beating beauty,
And only place a small part of myself
On the lobes to let myself fester naturally in the veins,
Or be snuffed out by disease
And either way I accept
For he is what has festered in my heart
But naturally, I will abide by what the natural order holds

~N. f.

Days in Recovery

1-

The beige and white borders callous me so
I am life's enemy, everyone knows
My foes are the light dancing in my mind
That I refuse to accept, but wish I could
For I do not want death to beckon me to
Ring my soul over just yet
Tooth and claw out of the jaws—
Death has not dutifully sent
A carriage for my precarious departure
I cling to the chains that have ridden me
And tear at their hinges
I may be horned down at the bellows
But my roar will not be drawn to silence
Before the light that guides thine eyes
to a promised land

2-

I didn't expect to find myself
On the hard memory foam mattress
When I rose this morning
I traced light fingertips on my wristband
And then my scars,
And thought it was all too unreal to be true
Yet, I got up, had breakfast, hugged those

Being discharged, hoping I could take their
Place, hugged my weeping mother with the
Visitors patch— I never thought I'd have to
See this sight— And witnessed
Two boys in the male unit beginning to
Behave incoherently
They rammed into doors, spreading paper down the
Hallway, ripped up everything in sight
Three hours, it was
Three hours, thirteen girls, one room containment
It was torment, but it happened
And now the hard mattress awaits my welcome

3-
I'm working well on my improvement
Status growing, I'm glowing
Across the unit, he likes me
I gave him my number, I hope he
Remembers to text me, but it's alright
He'll probably forget, and even if he might
I'm the happiest I've been in a while
So other people's actions will have no impact
On how I stand
I have grown stronger in these days
And have almost healed

We learned mindfulness, boundaries, helping
Skills, friendships, and positive affirmations
All in one day, and I don't feel manic,
But I feel elated and well
I have conquered my demons
And all I have to do is fly away from
My chains
Into blissful freedom

4-

The dark has submerged; I am as clean as
holy water on the fingertips of the Lord
My benefits induce me to stay a while
Longer, sure, but ensures my light will
Brighten for a lengthened time
I won't crumble behind iron bards yet
My feathers won't shroud amongst my wings
I will break free indefinitely
And I will never come back
None of us will

5-
I am in debt to those who've carried me
to where I am today
Alive, and in good health,
In love and fair way

For it is too early to tell
Where this song might lead
But I know pain well
Like an acquaintance I gaze upon
Every once in a blood moon
My shoulder for every wrong
A familiar countenance I presume
But only a hand I hold
A thought I no longer loom
For I have an artillery
To battle all my pain
A family to shield my fears
And a stronghold to prevent the rain
I have blossomed for years
And bloom I will continue everyday
For this place held my hand n' ear
And this sanction I shall never replace
6-
The day has come!
It arrived late, and sluggish, but no matter
The appearance— she's here
And to take me away to the next
Step of my recovery
I may be slightly reluctant to

Take her hand for the sake of this
Being a mistake, but I wonderfully
Accept her grasp as she will lead on
Heart felt and heavy
I shall move on

~N. f.

3.

You are

contempt

You are worth

it

You have lived

It is without prevail
I shall take my coat and live
In Alaskan mountains,
Then stroll to the buzzing hum of
Hollywood traffic courses
And renounce these built up fortress
Iron bars beneath my skin
In my homeland praries
The time I shall alter my world
With the path of another
Will only be to order my coffee
Then settle on a new adventure
To cascade in my wildest dreams

~N. f.

We are not a sob story
For the statistics
To stack up
We are not the outlier
In this community
We are the people who thrive
And are the future of this country
We have not been educated
To file into cubicles;
We were destined to
Break free from the chains
Of traditional thought
And lead the world
To a future we see fit
For the future boys and girls
To never become
Statistics again
    —*Teenagers are humans, too*

    ~N. f.

It has been a year without you

The first week I was heaved over the toilet
So physically in pain I couldn't stomach anything
And lost twelve pounds

The first month I was in denial that you
Didn't love me
That you spent nights
Sneaking around and mistaking my trust
For permission to do so

Four months in I still had pains in my stomach
Every time I saw you pass by
Yearning for one more day
One more hug
To feel safe in your arms again
To feel something
And instead found that something
In other men who didn't even look at me
The way you used to

Six months in and my therapy was going well
I was getting the much needed help
And was working through my pain
By working on myself
Writing to my heart's content
All the sad and lonely poetry I wanted

To drown out your voice in the night

Seven months in I published my first book
Detailing my life and the lessons
I picked up along the way
The growth I've made all packed into that spine of
A masterpiece
Of you
That I would learn later helped hundreds of men and
women
Learn to love themselves, too

Eight months in the semester ended
The sun was welcoming under the bells of
The graduation ceremony
And for the first time in months I felt content
With the peace the day brought to me

Eleven months in I have seen you quite often
As friends, in groups, we've laughed
And adventured to our best life
With the best foot forward
One night, we even kissed
I didn't feel uneasy
I didn't even feel pain
It happened so naturally that it felt like we were back
To our mischief eleven months ago
And I even felt content

To share another memory with you

Now twelve months have struck
I don't sense your ghost haunting me
Or me wondering what I did wrong
I know it was neither of us
That did anything wrong
For I loved you with all my heart
And part of me will always hold a place
For the first person I fell in love with
I have learned to be more independent
Intelligent with my heart
And involuntarily in love with myself
And the world around me
Through words, work, and kindness for all

~N. f.

I didn't think of loving you
It just naturally slipped in
Like if I loved you for my
Entire life

~N. f.

The light in her eyes
The adventure lurking
Just around the corner
Was searching for her

~N. f.

We are hoping
To rise above this
Ash whole
And newborn

~N. f.

"What is she doing?"
She is blooming

~N. f.

The calamity
Of closeness to the rocky ground
And the smirking ocean skies
Keeps my unbound body at bay
The wind writing soft melodies
Overturning the depression of the night
Stark, regal, overpowering pools of black
Fully bubbled with heavy anticipation
To wash out morning dew
The protectors of the nature
Envies the ones who can hear
The soft hum of God
In the willow trees
And carry out His will
In graceful motions of conducting,
Swaying their palms with the beat
Of his message through poetry
And contemporary art
That shall only present sanity
To those who hear his wishes
In the buzzing corridors aside humanity

~N. f.

If life be presumed so ardent
And the labors prove abhorrent
In the slow release of passion
That I, mind you, would never find
Struck away from the path of redeeming glory
When the effusion of my present self
Seems so neglectful of the dream to be
I adhere myself to study, and in such,
Refuge grows as the roots of knowledge
Capsize the mind, and age thy soul
I am ethereal in my steps
And no being present could deter
The love, all this love, I effuse so proudly
Will they never comprehend,
But fasten so detrimentally
I hold no other truth to my rigors
But to be in the motions infallibly
Eternally, and gracefully

~N. f.

The petals that fall from the rose
Will only give the chance to grow a garden
And once planted,
You will just have to watch

~N. f.

And what if the world
Fell in love with you?

~N. f.

The longing will shorten
And the memories will distance
The pain will be forgiven
And the love will listen

~N. f.

The mind is wandering
For the essence is calamity
In the face of promising love
Lingering with tiptoe waltz
I chill to temper, so temperate
With the smile to soothe
A sigh, swing softly so that I sound
So sweet and solid
To a bond I reinforce
With yellow bands, pink ribbon
In a bow I take
For its glory

~N. f.

I want to be in love with you enough
For the poetry to be enough
To even make the cold fall in love
I want to fall in love
With the way you breathe
And smile
And laugh
So I may only write about that
Never again the lonely corridors
But to all into eternal happiness
Never again trapped by the thorns
Of longing for a lover to appeal well

~N. f.

She danced with the wind
In her hair and the Earth
At her gentle fingers
Spreading nurture and blooming
Wherever she graced
This is how she loved, too,
Never to welt under the shadows
Never to die in the moonlight
Never to question the beauty of nature
She loved ethereally and passion
Greeted her at every frozen corner
She didn't question why
She just lived

~N. f.

He became her stars
To watch her flowers bloom from afar
He became the water
To her roots and to never let her starve
For she craved the love like life itself
And she wasn't alone anymore
She had him at her side

~N. f.

Her vision cleared before him
He wiped away her tears
It was love she didn't believe in
But he stripped her of all of her fears
She had loved before
But he was a figure different
She was no longer shrouded in the darkness
There was life and love still to be
There was hope she wasn't alone
He would stand, stay, and walk with me

~N. f.

And who are they to say
What our fate is?
We live together to grow
As I have faith in him

~N. f.

Love the love you love
There is no other way to live
Than to love

~N. f.

He smelled of adventures in the midnight moonlight,
Meaning no more monotonous
Tongue could ever speak in the presence
Of his soul

~N. f.

Thank you for diving deep
Into my soul
You ignited the words
That will now never stop flowing
But not for you
Anyone else but *you* now

~N. f.

I have loved far more
Than even the most romantic
Would fall in love with me

~N. f.

You are everything
I've been looking for
In a soul mate
We match as we've lived
Hundreds of lives
Together

~N. f.

I absentmindedly
    Idle between the thoughts
        Of you

~N. f.

He laughed so pure
That even the angels swooned
A love that would forever endure
Dusk, to dawn, to noon
I wish only to recieve the kindness
Of his soul to be my reprise
The gleaming blue of his eyes
To be what I long for everyday to
His brooding hands to caress my
Bruised, hungry fingertips
To make me fall more with time
As long as our love has already kindled
A world where we both confide to
Each other and in harmony we live
A path we gracefully step
So we never leave

~N. f.

he is peacefully drifting off
to a dream so sweet
his lips still faintly
are curled with delight
maybe he is reliving
a cheerful moment
or fabricating a new one
i am dreaming of him
in a new life
away from the chaos
away from the lingering distress
and into a veranda home
filled with light
and love
and most importantly
a dream
i can live amongst besides
him
where we don't have to escape
in our slumber
and can play it through
everyday
as if it were our heaven
in a little pocket of earth

~ N. f.

I live for a love like this
Eternally and sealed with his kiss

~N. f.

You need to know the love
For yourselves is not lost
To others when they don't
Return the beauty you gift

~N. f.

We must reconnect with our roots
The stars
To console our souls from pain
Then, and only then,
Shall we bloom

~N. f.

Know that there will be rough
Waters to your beautiful glistening
Stream
There will be times the currents
Become rocky with uncertainty
To the forks in the way, splitting
Your future into the unknown
Yet you will reach the sea
And drift out into the wildest of dreams

~N. f.

Music touches the soul
Poetry mends the heart
Laughter clears the mind
Joy brings hate to an end
A song so love will start

~N. f.

When I make my way to the sky
I do not look at the clouds and wonder
Why I'm not the same shade as them
The pink and blue hues
Do not phase my yellow shine
As I soar
And I bring some along with me
For all deserve to rise higher
And view the magnificent world underneath
Our stardust

~N. f.

I want to love you enough
To write a love song that will sing
As proudly as I am to be with you
And I'd hope you'd hum along

~N. f.

there's something that makes
the growth of the sun
in the morning
that makes me shine,
too

~ *N. f.*

There will be people
Who don't like the way you
Rule your world
Or your thrown
Or your duties
To protect your fortress
But that's why it was made for you
And you alone
Your castle is magnificent
Don't let the passerbyers
Criticize the walls
Without knowing what's inside

~N. f.

And that smile
I could have loved that smile
In a thousand other life times
If it were destiny to find one another

~N. f.